Surviving The Dust Bowl

By Jo Cleland
Illustrated By Pete McDonnell

ROURKE PUBLISHING

Vero Beach, Florida 32964

www.rourkepublishing.com

Edited by Katherine M. Thal
Illustrated by Pete McDonnell
Art Direction and Page Layout by Renee Brady

Library of Congress Cataloging-in-Publication Data

Cleland, Joann.
  Surviving the Dust Bowl / Jo Cleland.
      p. cm. -- (Eye on history graphic illustrated)
  Includes bibliographical references and index.
  ISBN 978-1-60694-441-7 (alk. paper)
  ISBN 978-1-60694-550-6 (soft cover)
  1. Dust Bowl Era, 1931-1939--Juvenile literature. 2. Dust storms--Great Plains--History--20th century--Juvenile literature. 3. Droughts--Great Plains--History--20th century--Juvenile literature. 4. Farmers--Great Plains--History--20th century--Juvenile literature. 5. Great Plains--History--20th century--Juvenile literature. 6. Middle West--History--20th century--Juvenile literature. I. Title.
  F595.C63 2010
  978'.032--dc22
                                    2009020502

Printed in the USA

CG/CG

www.rourkepublishing.com - rourke@rourkepublishing.com
Post Office Box 643328 Vero Beach, Florida 32964

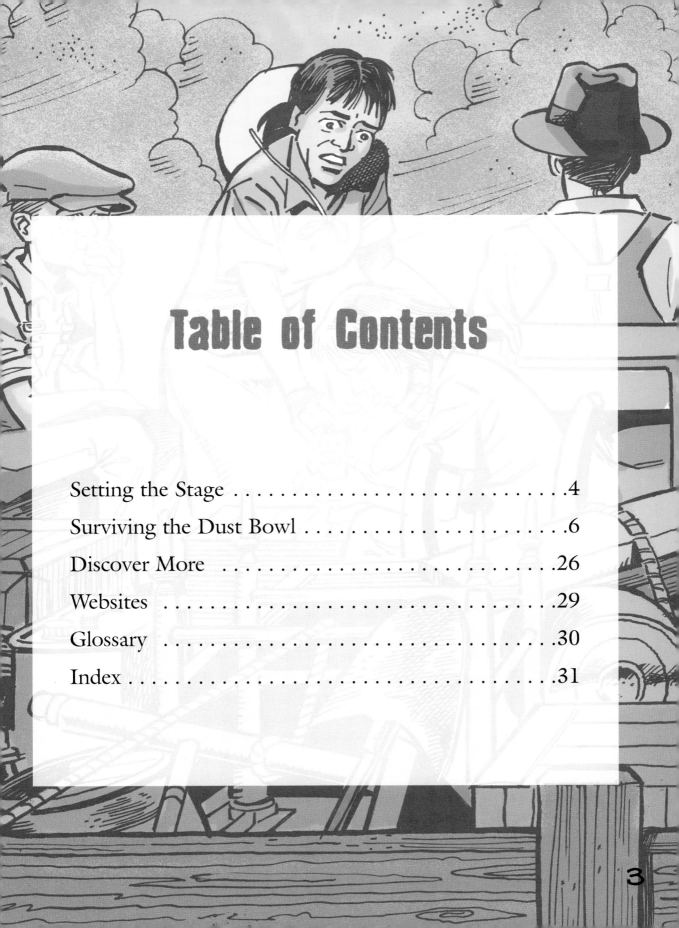

Table of Contents

THE OKLAHOMA SUN

Sunday

Issue 5   Volume 12

July 12th, 1935

Families Flee As Another Dust Storm Blankets The Midwest! Many Run

At least three million families have fled their homes and farms on the Great Plains during what has been called the worst worldwide environmental disaster of the twentieth century. The 1930s drought has forced many families to migrate to the West and to other states in search of food and fresh water. This environmental disaster is a result of a lack of precipitation and poor farming practices, which have caused the soil to become dry and airborne. Clearly, the Midwest has become an uninhabitable dust bowl.

This Texas town looks like a ghost town as a wall of dust approaches during a dust storm in 1935.

From the period of 1930 to 1939, dust storms devastated large parts of Kansas, Oklahoma, Texas, Colorado, and New Mexico. The areas affected by the dust storms became known as the Dust Bowl.

Huge rolling walls of dust forced hundreds of thousands of families to hurriedly pack their belongings, leaving their homes and farms behind to be buried under a blanket of dust.

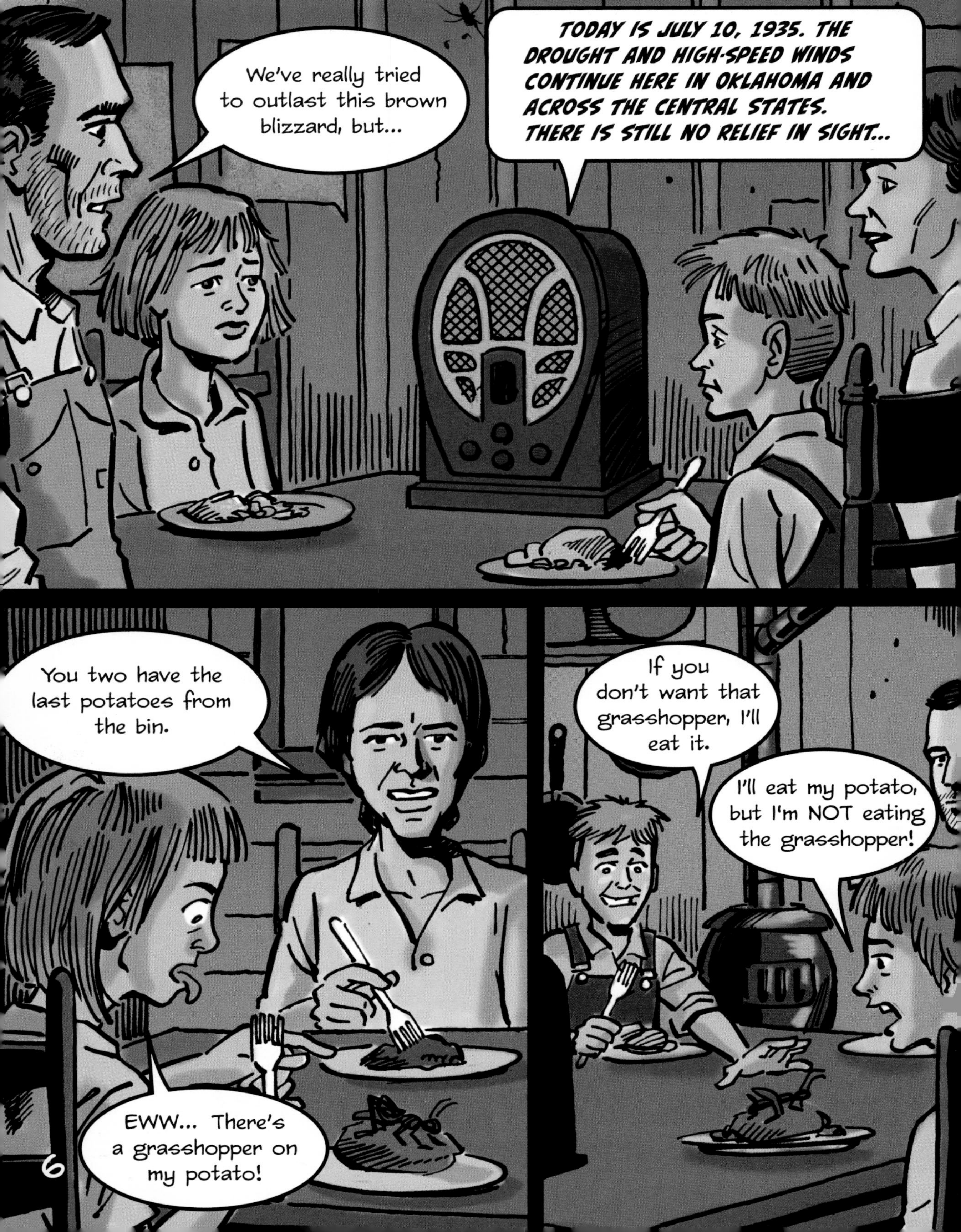
We've really tried to outlast this brown blizzard, but...
TODAY IS JULY 10, 1935. THE DROUGHT AND HIGH-SPEED WINDS CONTINUE HERE IN OKLAHOMA AND ACROSS THE CENTRAL STATES. THERE IS STILL NO RELIEF IN SIGHT...
You two have the last potatoes from the bin.
EWW... There's a grasshopper on my potato!
If you don't want that grasshopper, I'll eat it.
I'll eat my potato, but I'm NOT eating the grasshopper!

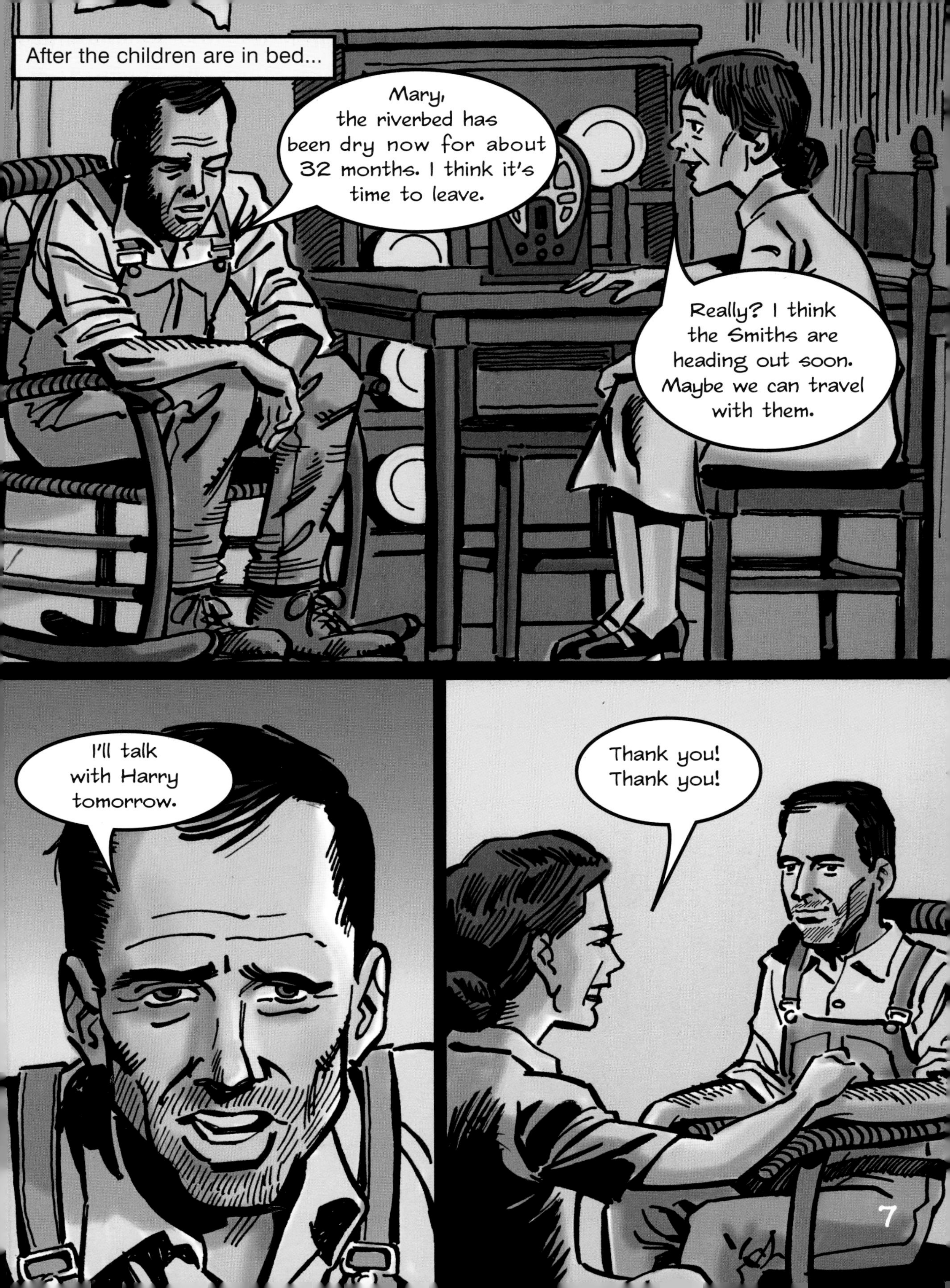
After the children are in bed...
Mary, the riverbed has been dry now for about 32 months. I think it's time to leave.
Really? I think the Smiths are heading out soon. Maybe we can travel with them.
I'll talk with Harry tomorrow.
Thank you! Thank you!

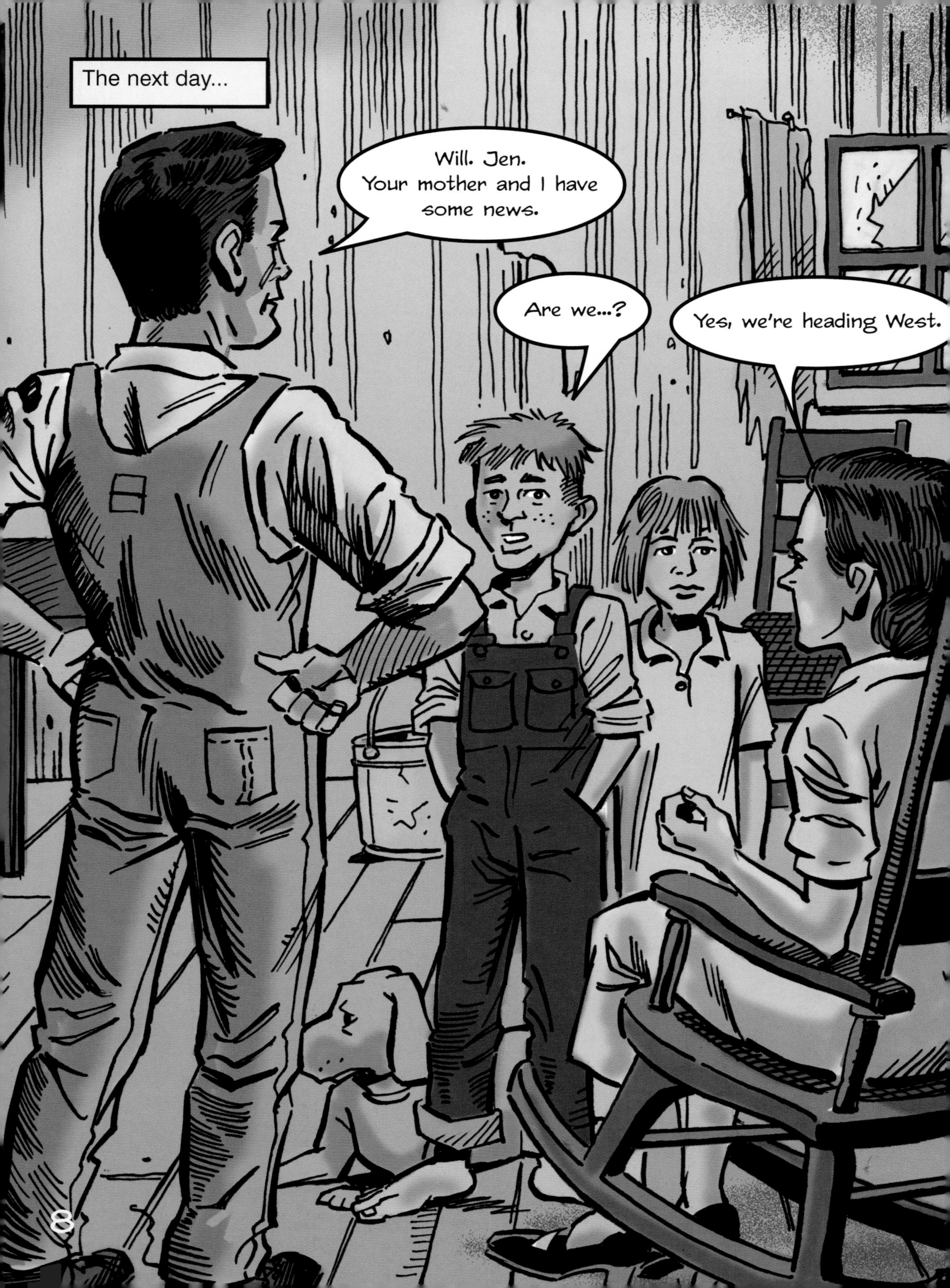
The next day...
Will. Jen. Your mother and I have some news.
Are we...?
Yes, we're heading West.

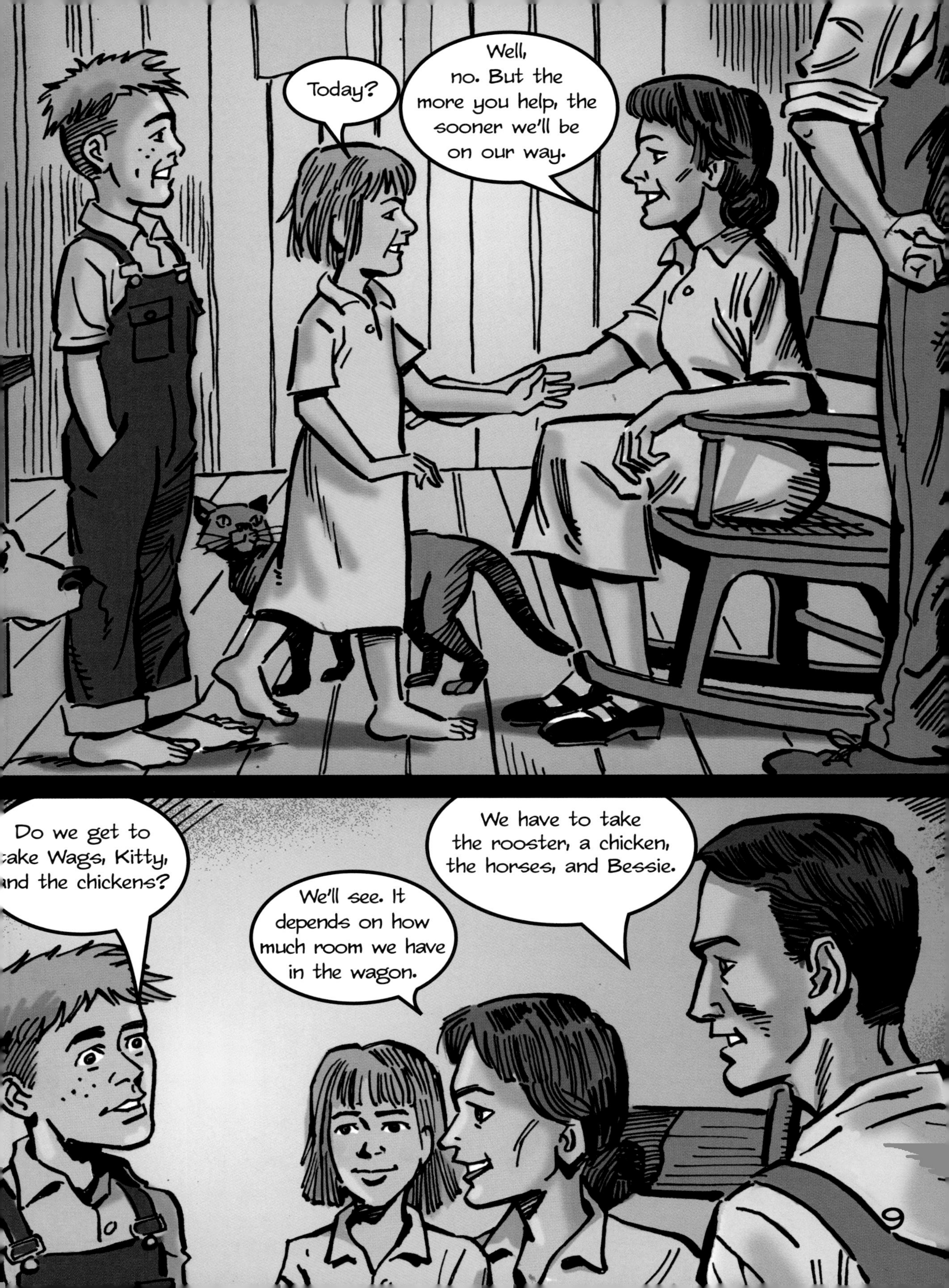
Today?
Well, no. But the more you help, the sooner we'll be on our way.
Do we get to ake Wags, Kitty, nd the chickens?
We have to take the rooster, a chicken, the horses, and Bessie.
We'll see. It depends on how much room we have in the wagon.

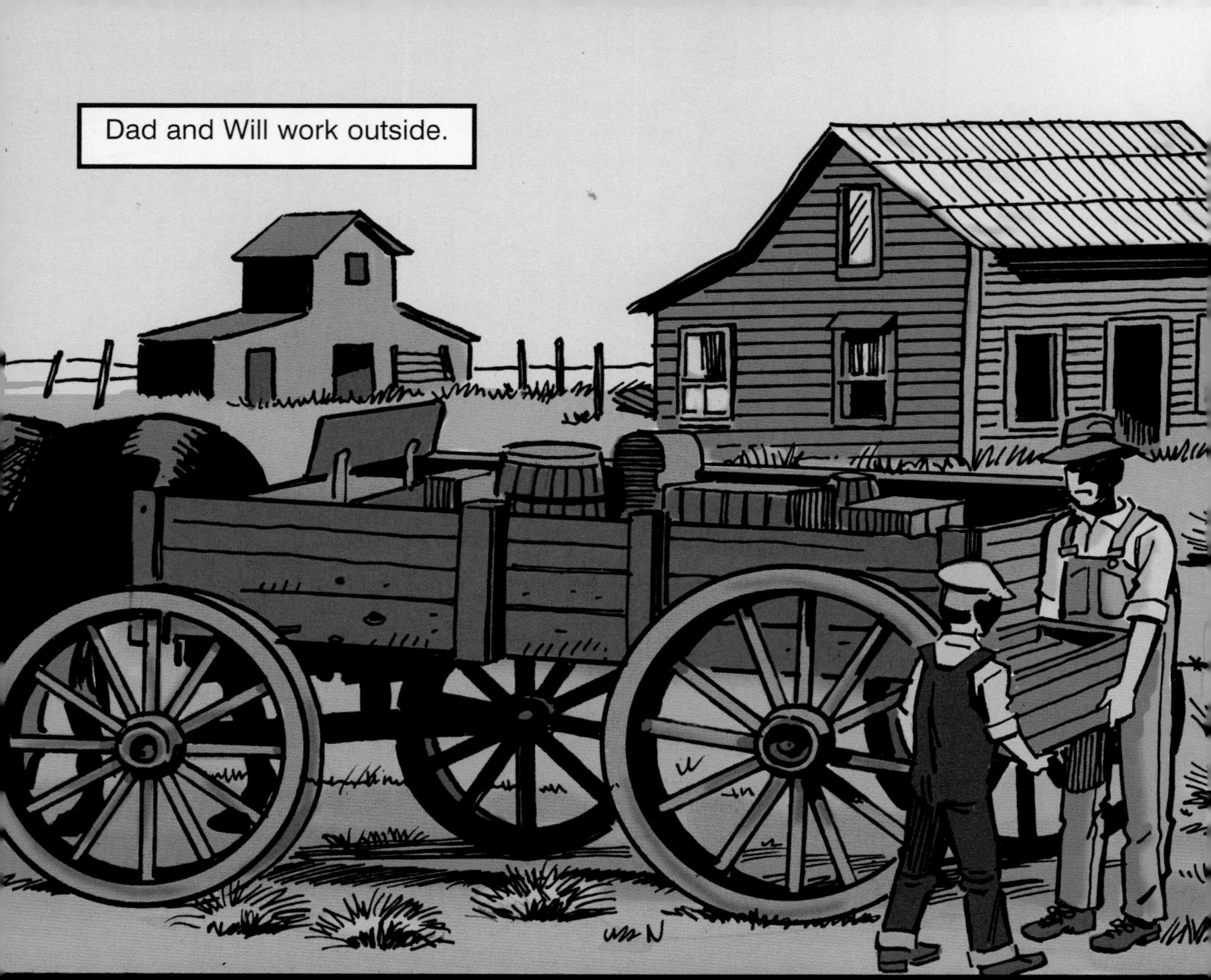
Dad and Will work outside.

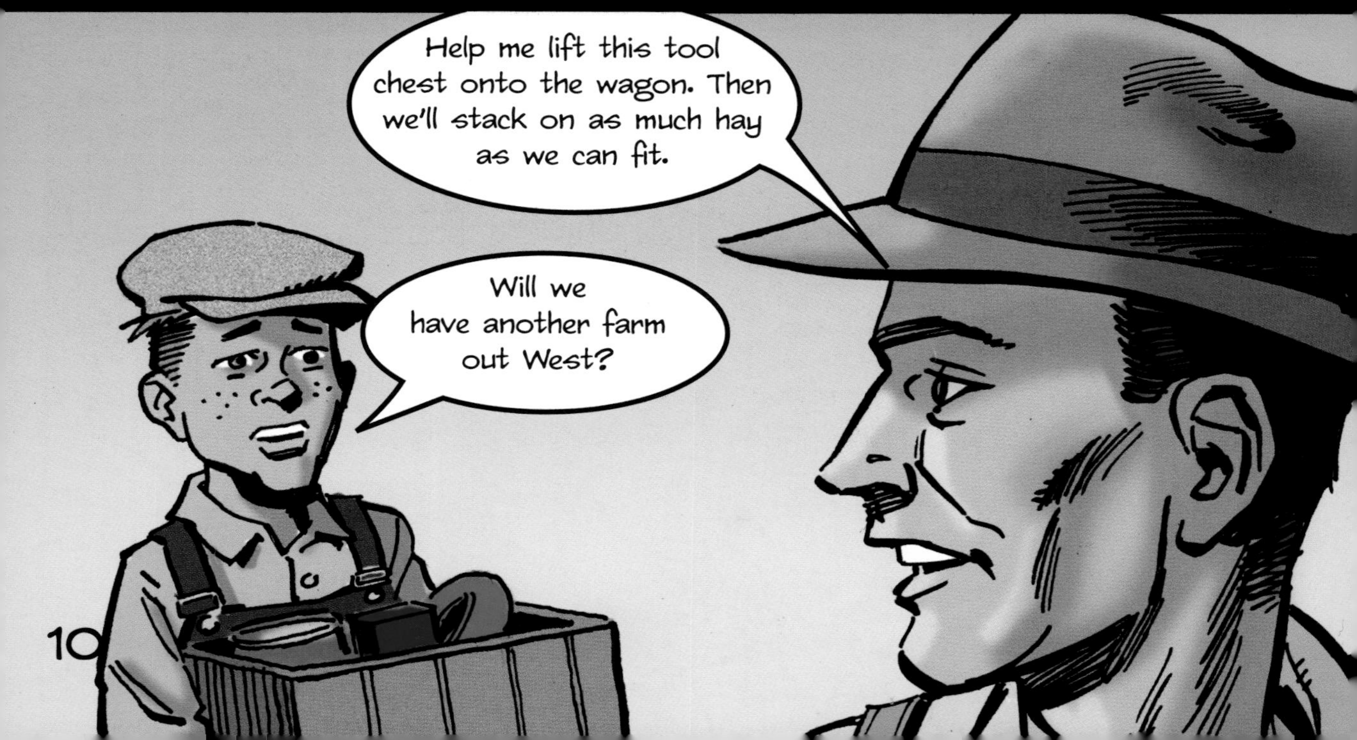
Help me lift this tool chest onto the wagon. Then we'll stack on as much hay as we can fit.
Will we have another farm out West?

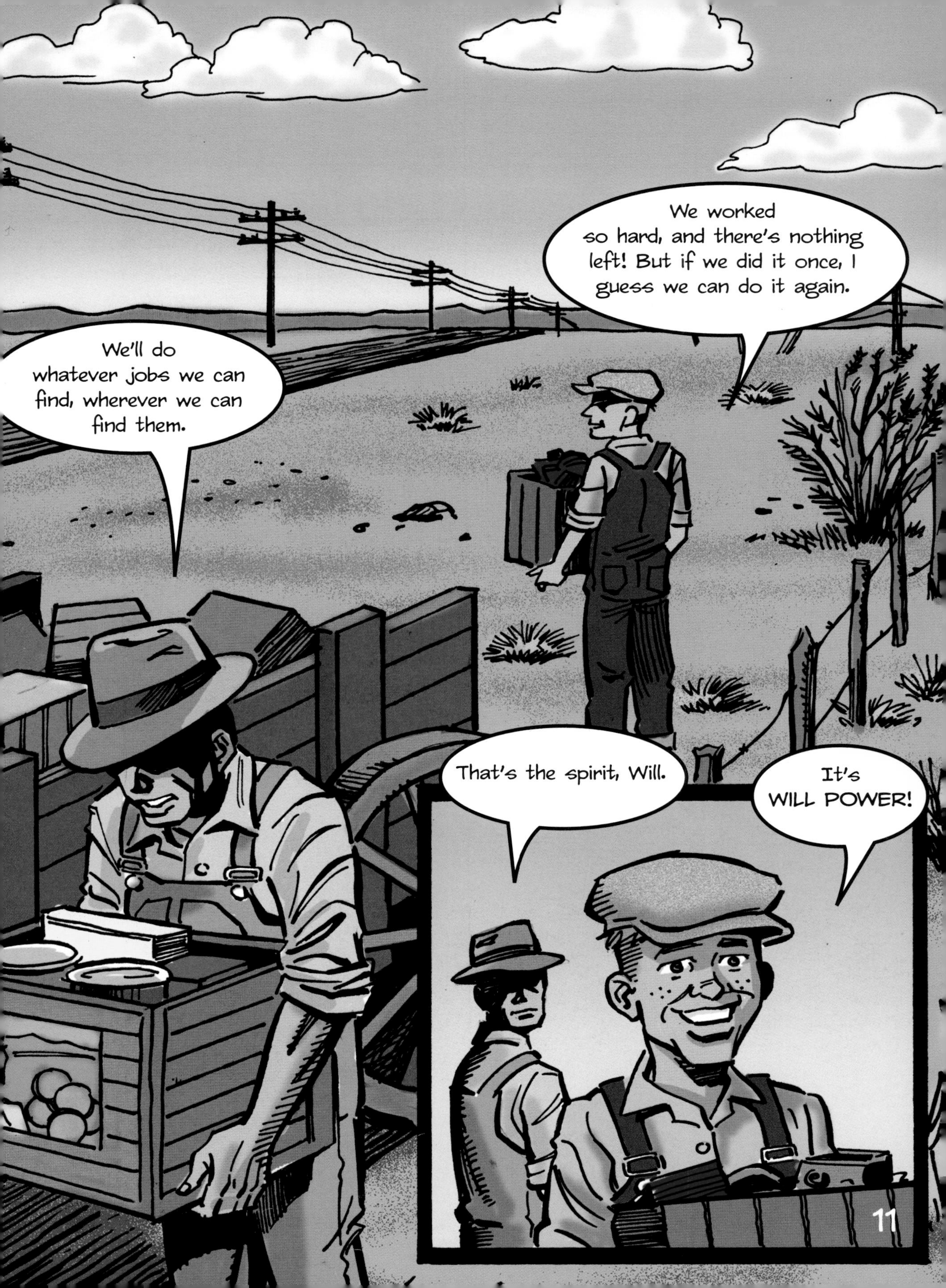
We'll do whatever jobs we can find, wherever we can find them.
We worked so hard, and there's nothing left! But if we did it once, I guess we can do it again.
That's the spirit, Will.
It's WILL POWER!

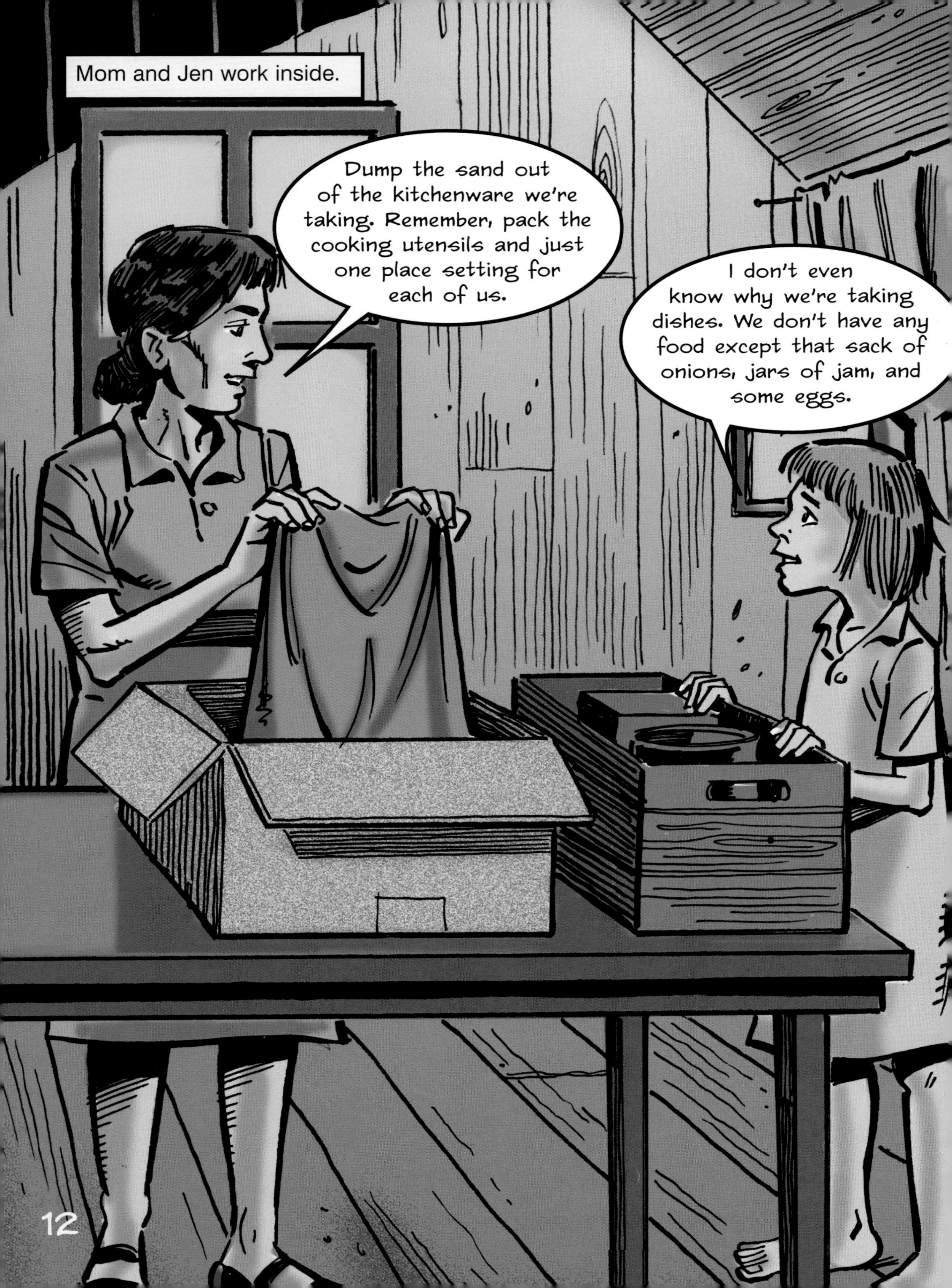
Mom and Jen work inside.
Dump the sand out of the kitchenware we're taking. Remember, pack the cooking utensils and just one place setting for each of us.
I don't even know why we're taking dishes. We don't have any food except that sack of onions, jars of jam, and some eggs.

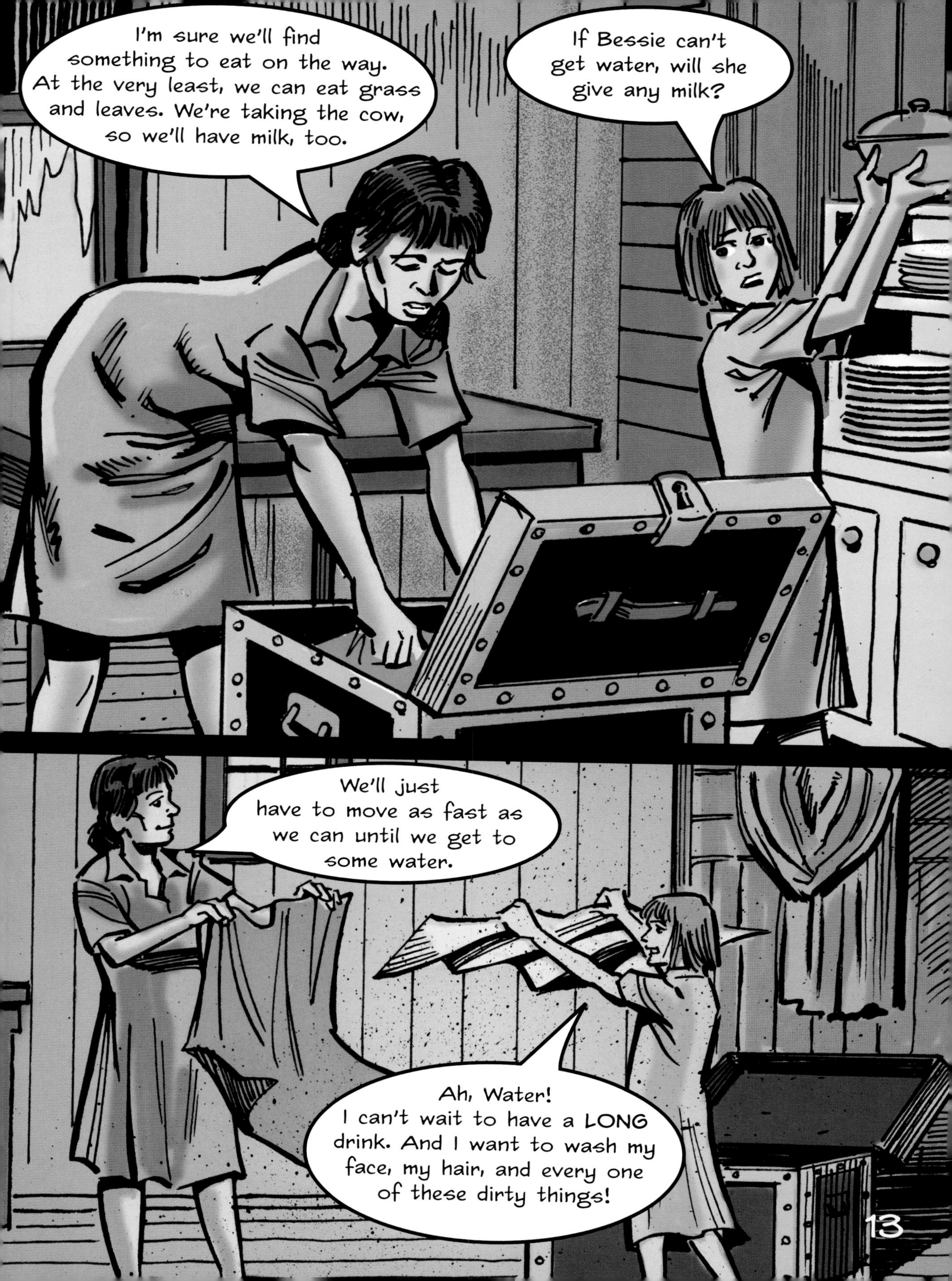
I'm sure we'll find something to eat on the way. At the very least, we can eat grass and leaves. We're taking the cow, so we'll have milk, too.
If Bessie can't get water, will she give any milk?
We'll just have to move as fast as we can until we get to some water.
Ah, Water! I can't wait to have a LONG drink. And I want to wash my face, my hair, and every one of these dirty things!

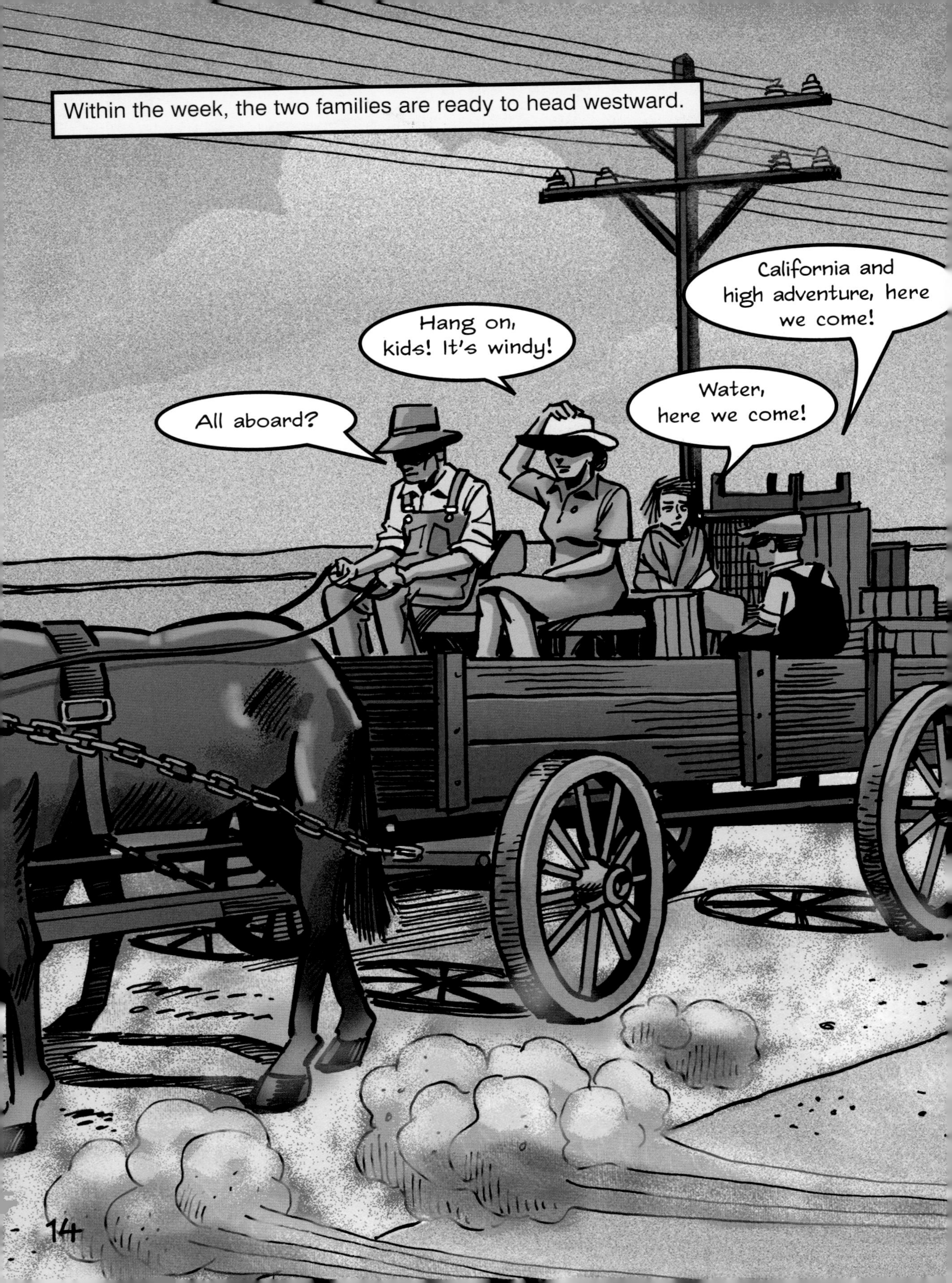
Within the week, the two families are ready to head westward.
All aboard?
Hang on, kids! It's windy!
Water, here we come!
California and high adventure, here we come!

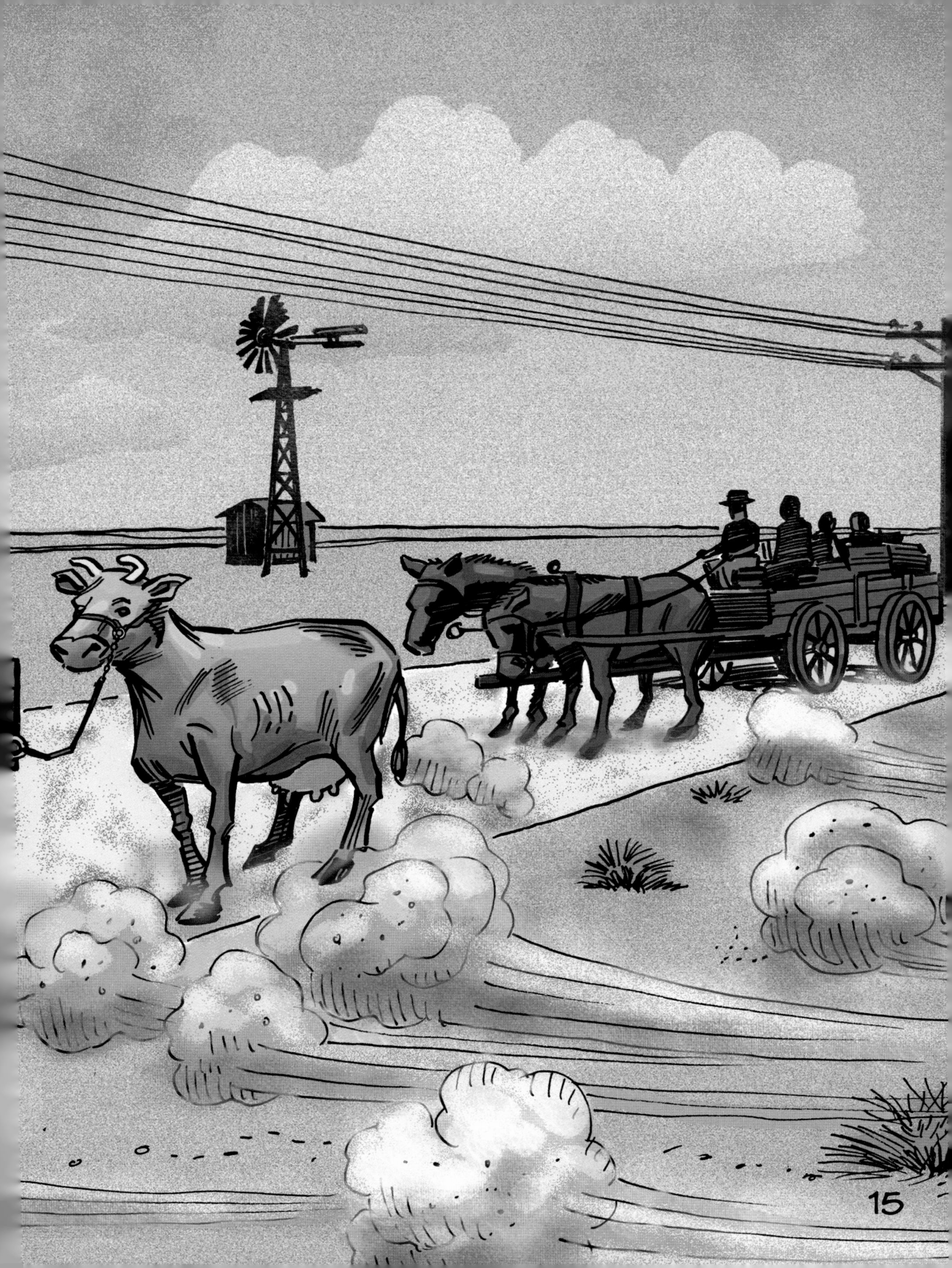

They have traveled less than a mile when Jen suddenly begins to cough and choke.

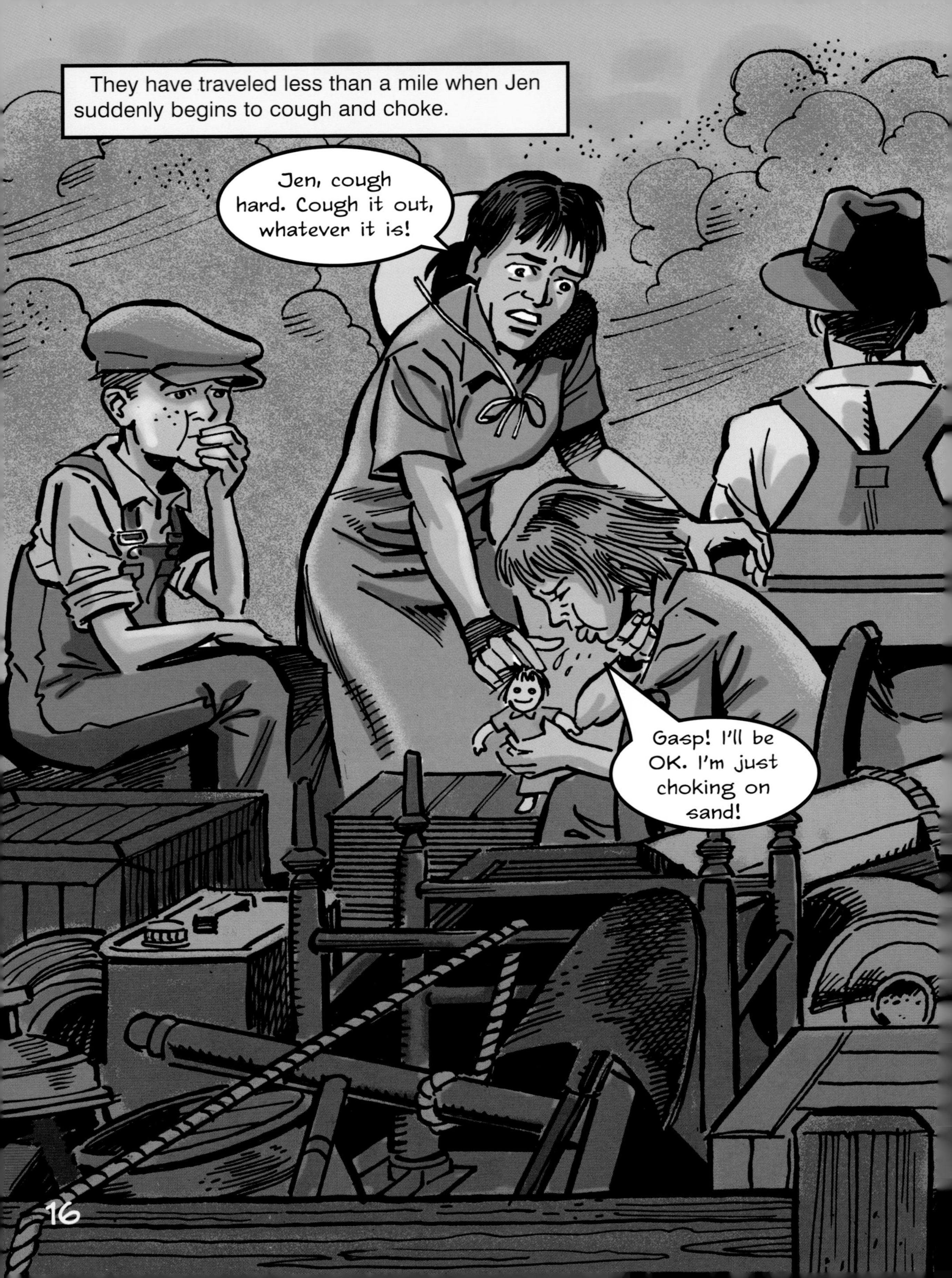

Jen, cough hard. Cough it out, whatever it is!
Gasp! I'll be OK. I'm just choking on sand!

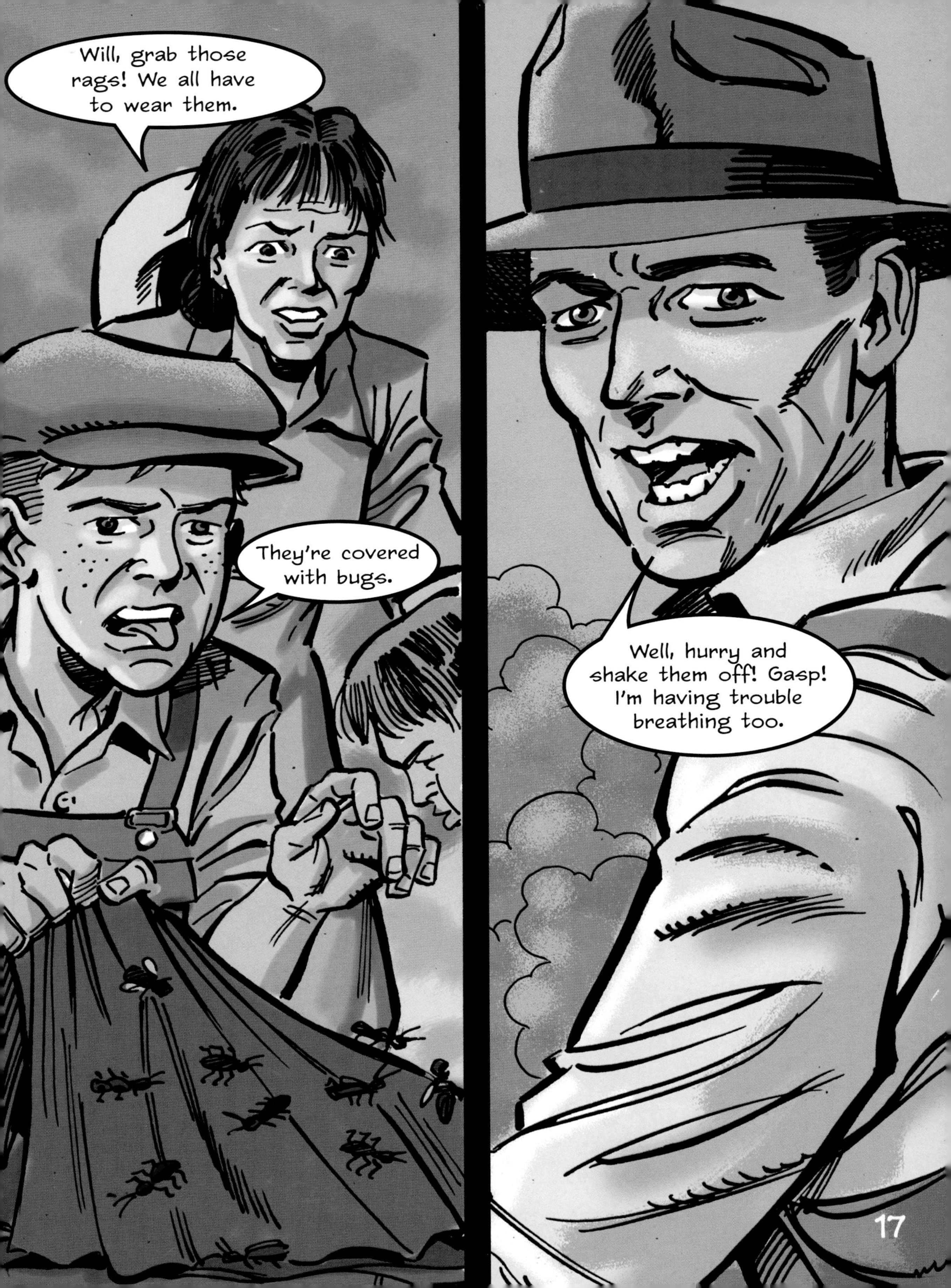
Will, grab those rags! We all have to wear them.
They're covered with bugs.
Well, hurry and shake them off! Gasp! I'm having trouble breathing too.

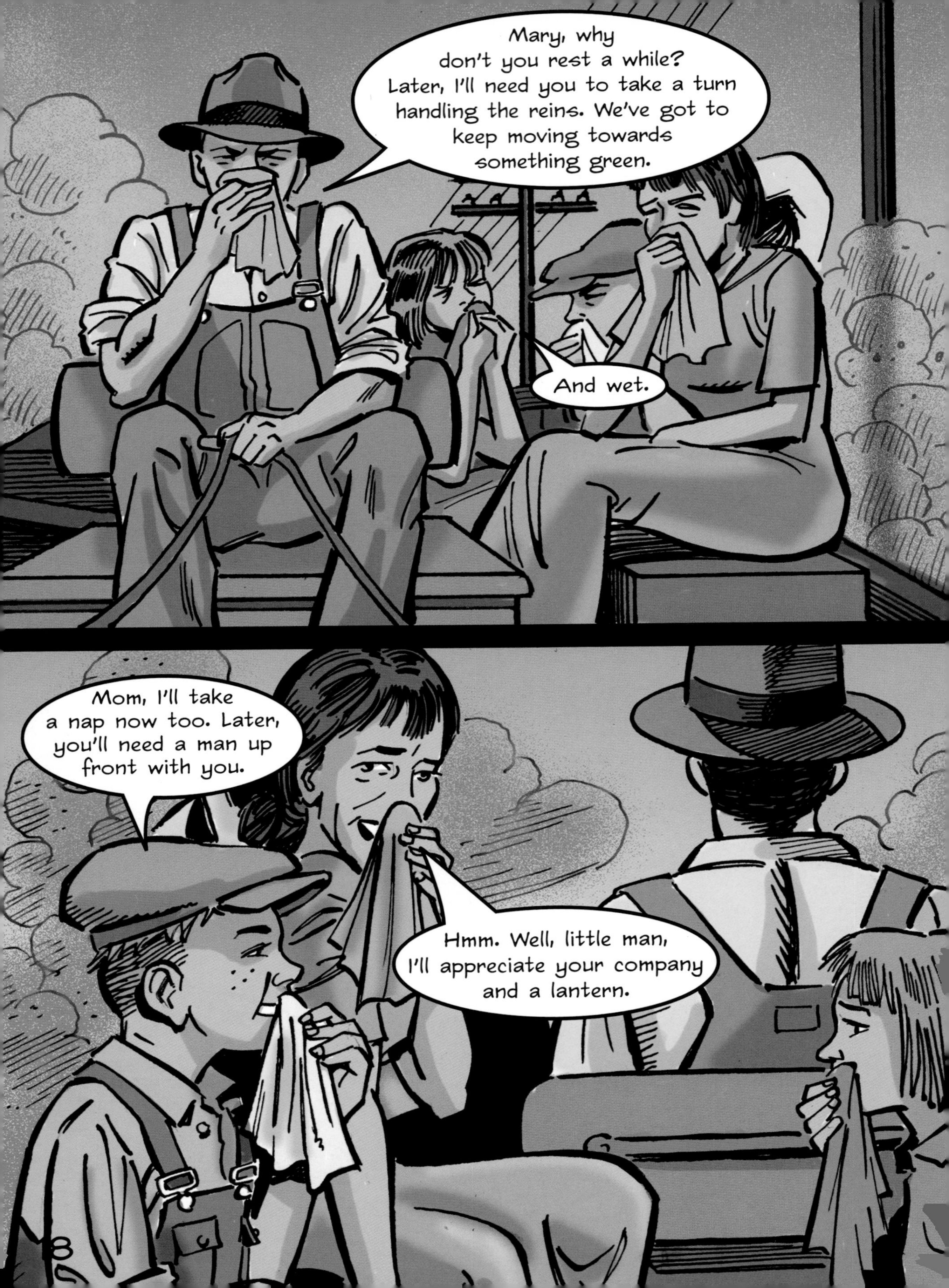
Mary, why don't you rest a while? Later, I'll need you to take a turn handling the reins. We've got to keep moving towards something green.
And wet.
Mom, I'll take a nap now too. Later, you'll need a man up front with you.
Hmm. Well, little man, I'll appreciate your company and a lantern.

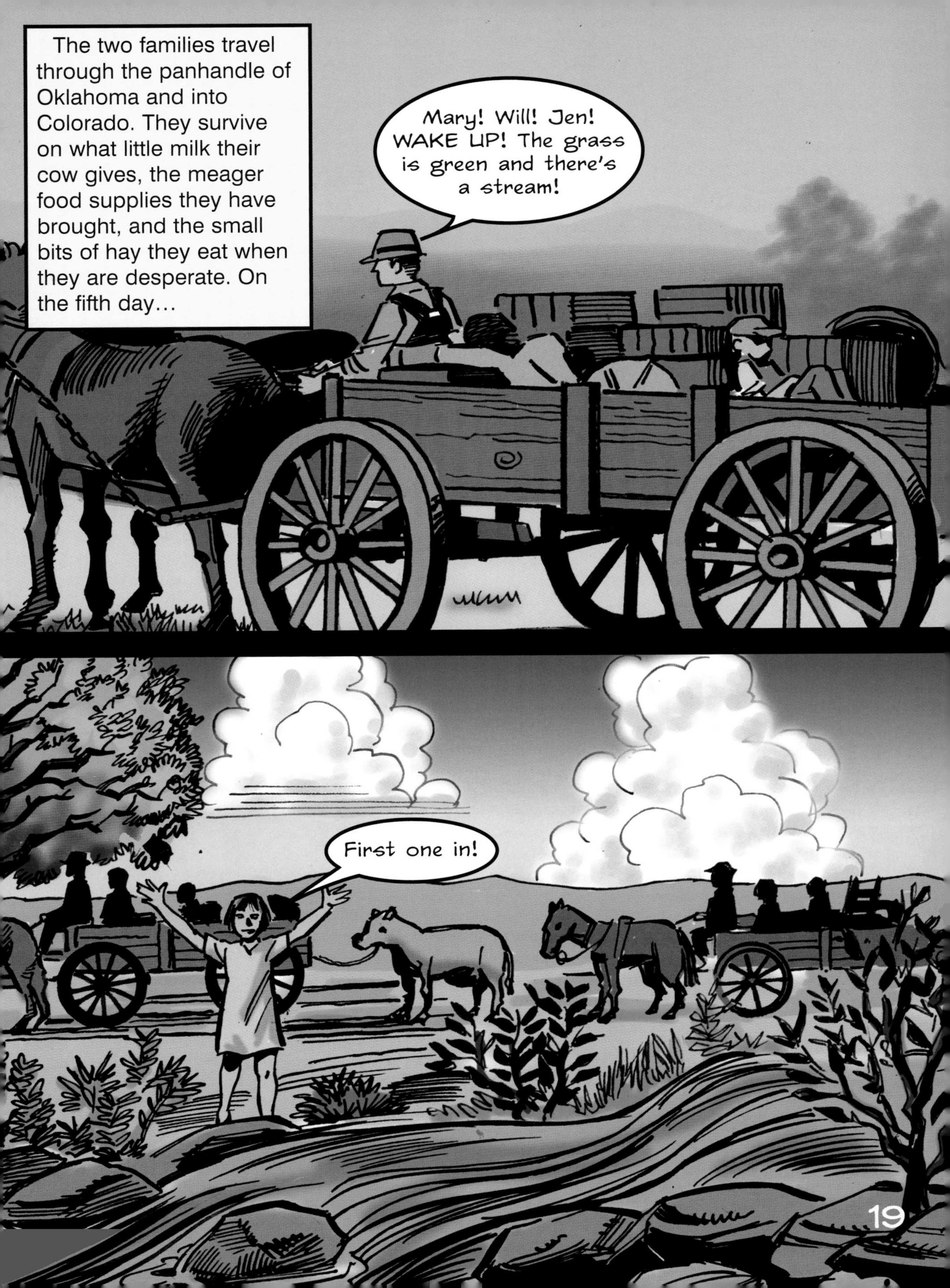
The two families travel through the panhandle of Oklahoma and into Colorado. They survive on what little milk their cow gives, the meager food supplies they have brought, and the small bits of hay they eat when they are desperate. On the fifth day…
Mary! Will! Jen! WAKE UP! The grass is green and there's a stream!
First one in!

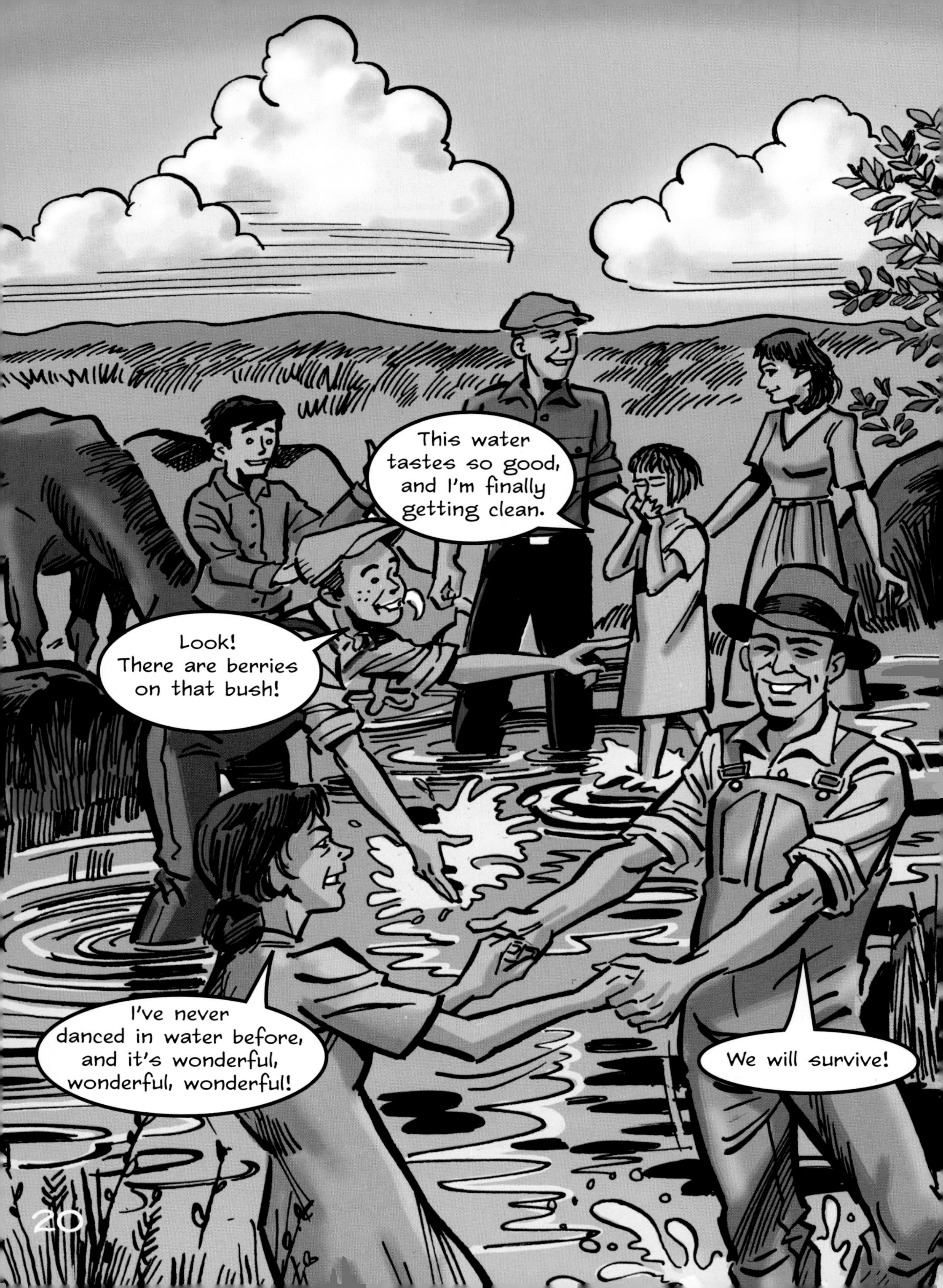
This water tastes so good, and I'm finally getting clean.
Look! There are berries on that bush!
I've never danced in water before, and it's wonderful, wonderful, wonderful!
We will survive!

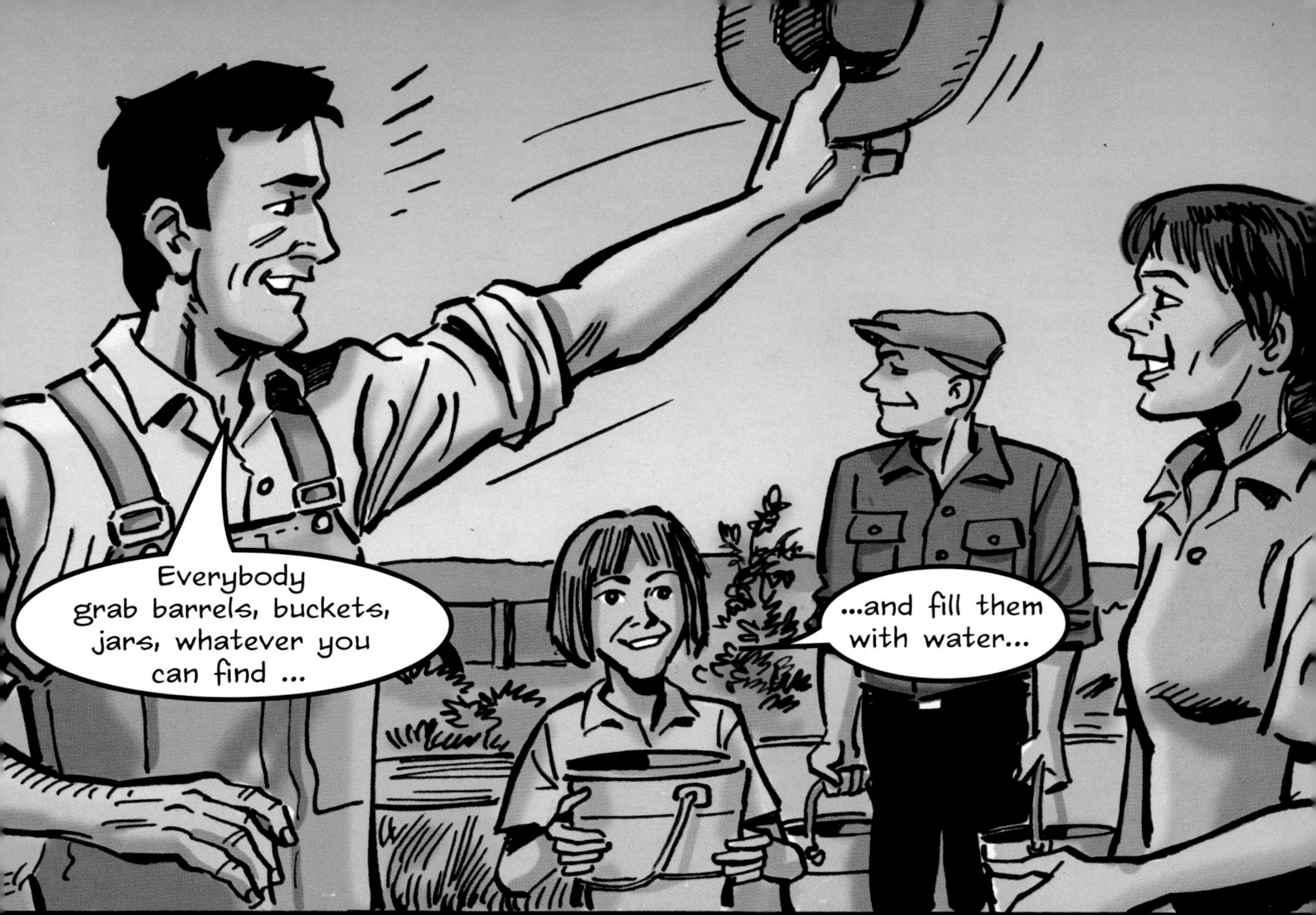
Everybody grab barrels, buckets, jars, whatever you can find ...
...and fill them with water...

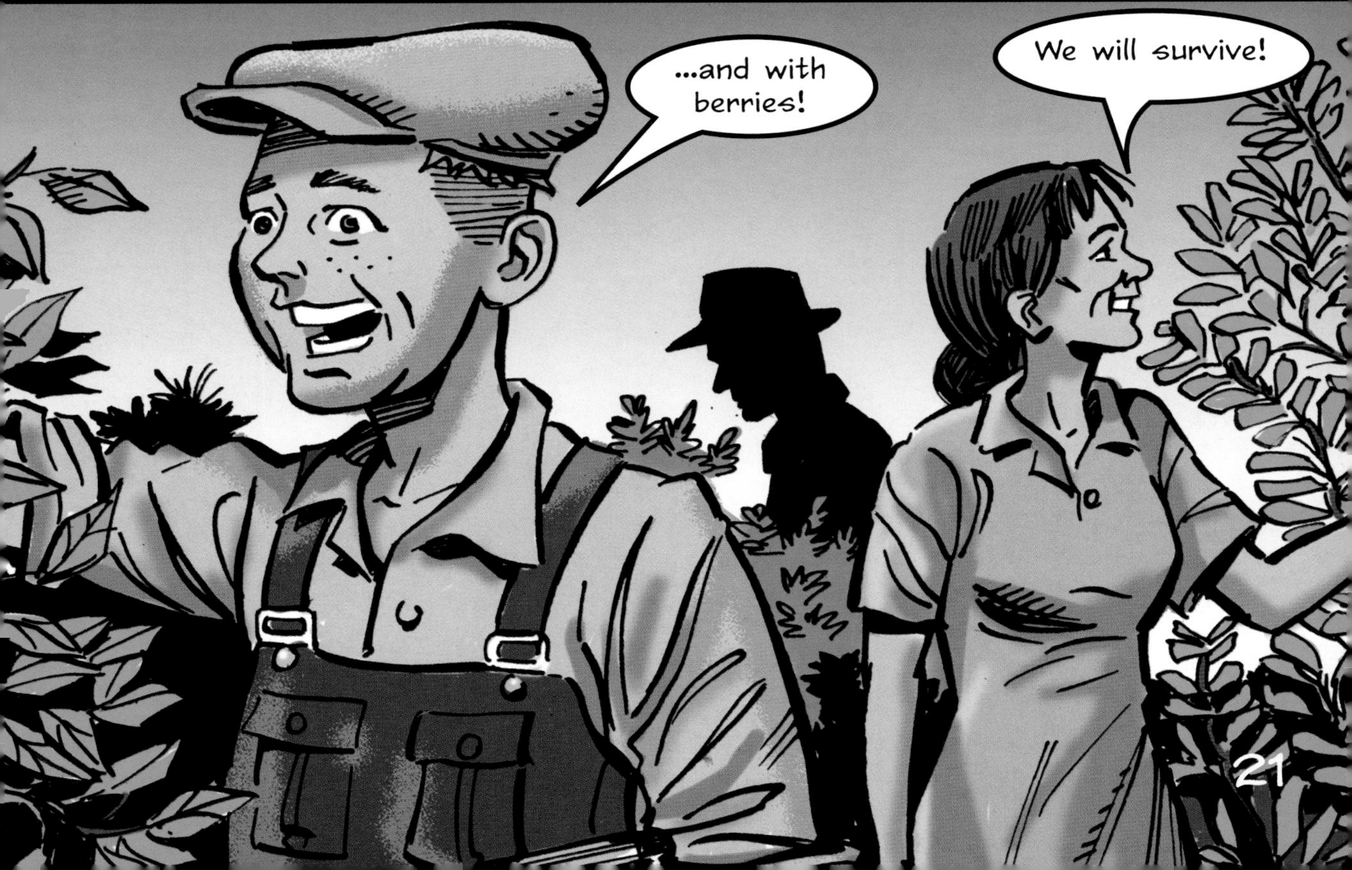
...and with berries!
We will survive!

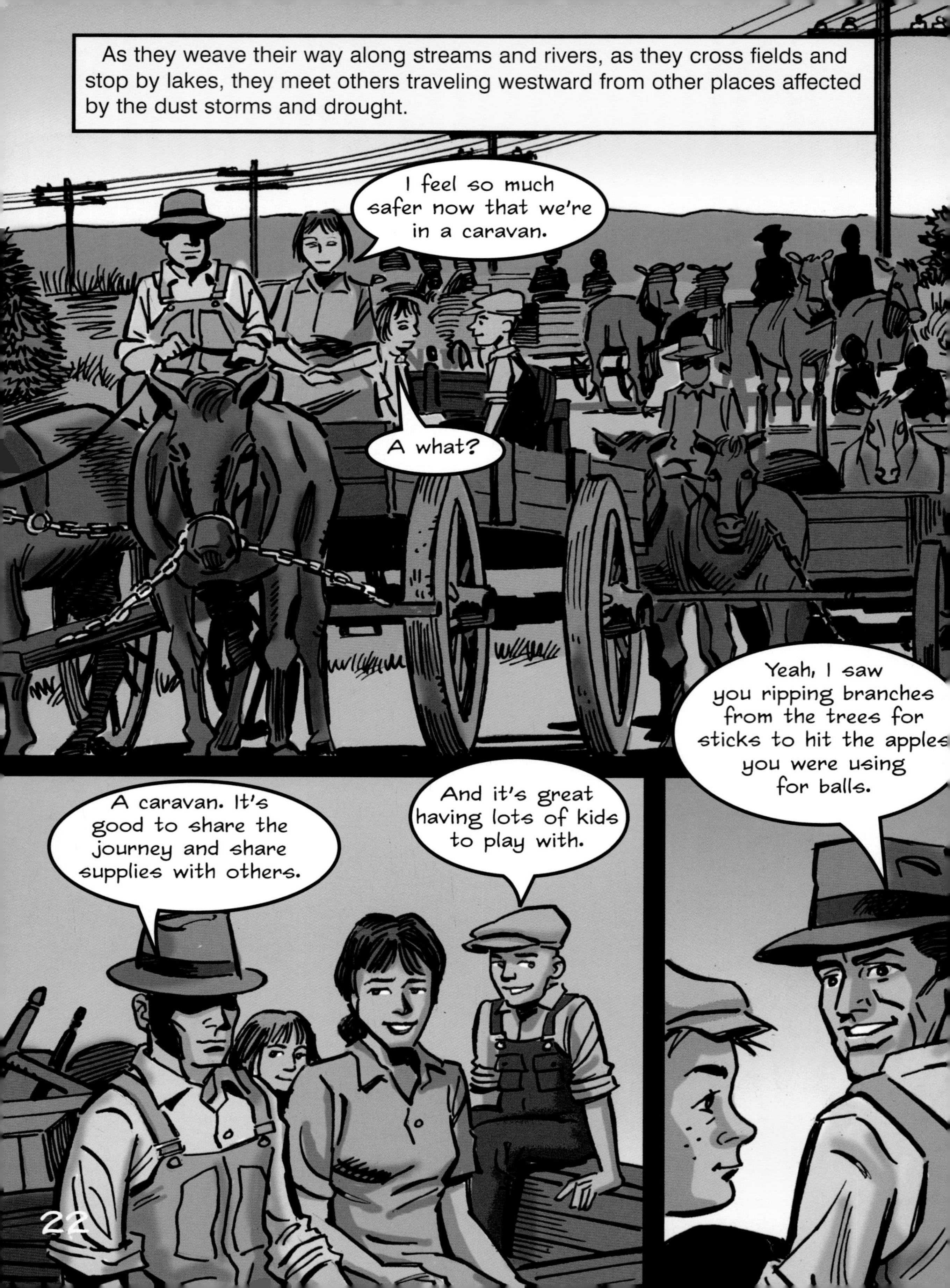
As they weave their way along streams and rivers, as they cross fields and stop by lakes, they meet others traveling westward from other places affected by the dust storms and drought.
I feel so much safer now that we're in a caravan.
A what?
A caravan. It's good to share the journey and share supplies with others.
And it's great having lots of kids to play with.
Yeah, I saw you ripping branches from the trees for sticks to hit the apples you were using for balls.

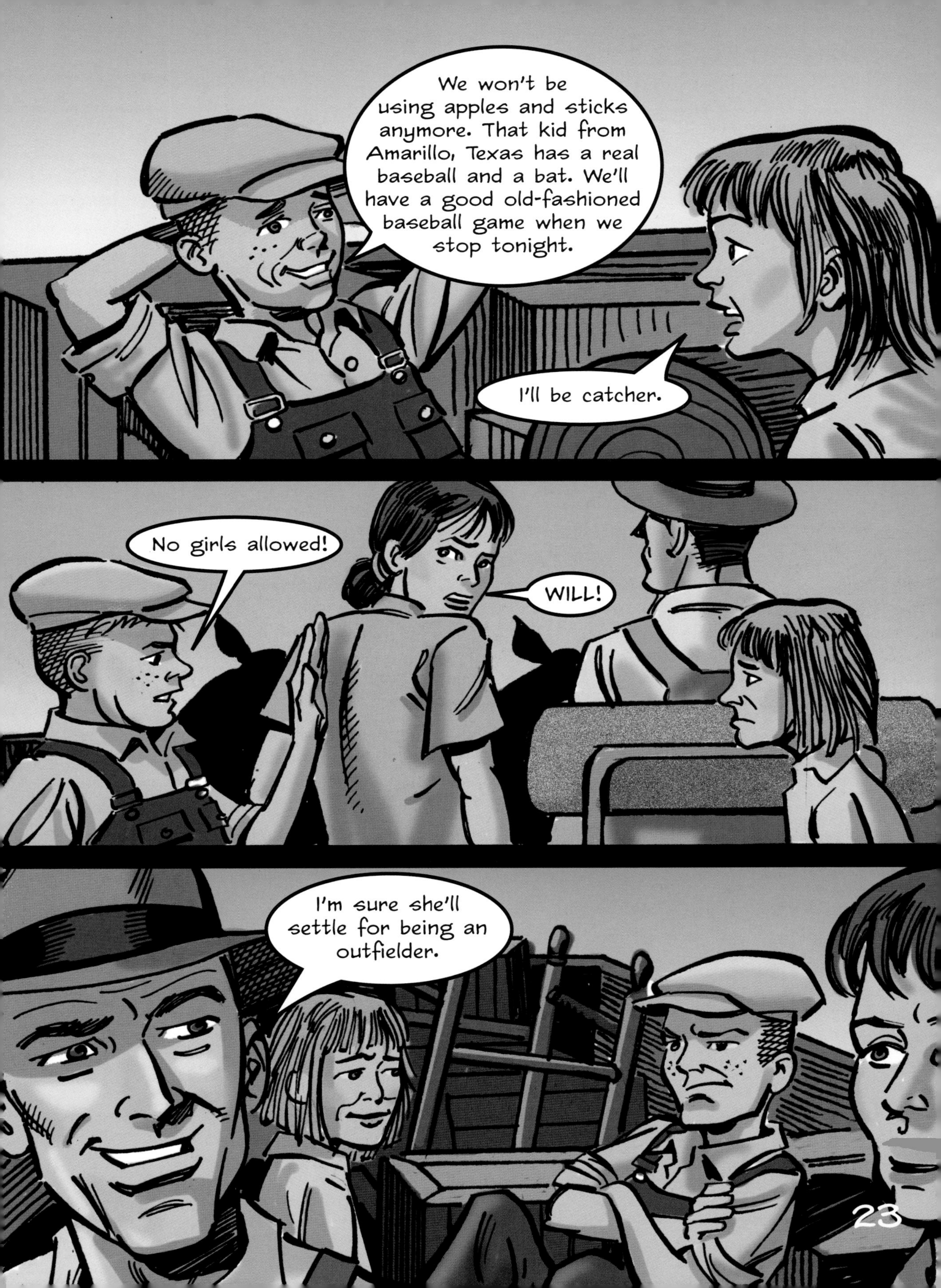
We won't be using apples and sticks anymore. That kid from Amarillo, Texas has a real baseball and a bat. We'll have a good old-fashioned baseball game when we stop tonight.
I'll be catcher.
No girls allowed!
WILL!
I'm sure she'll settle for being an outfielder.

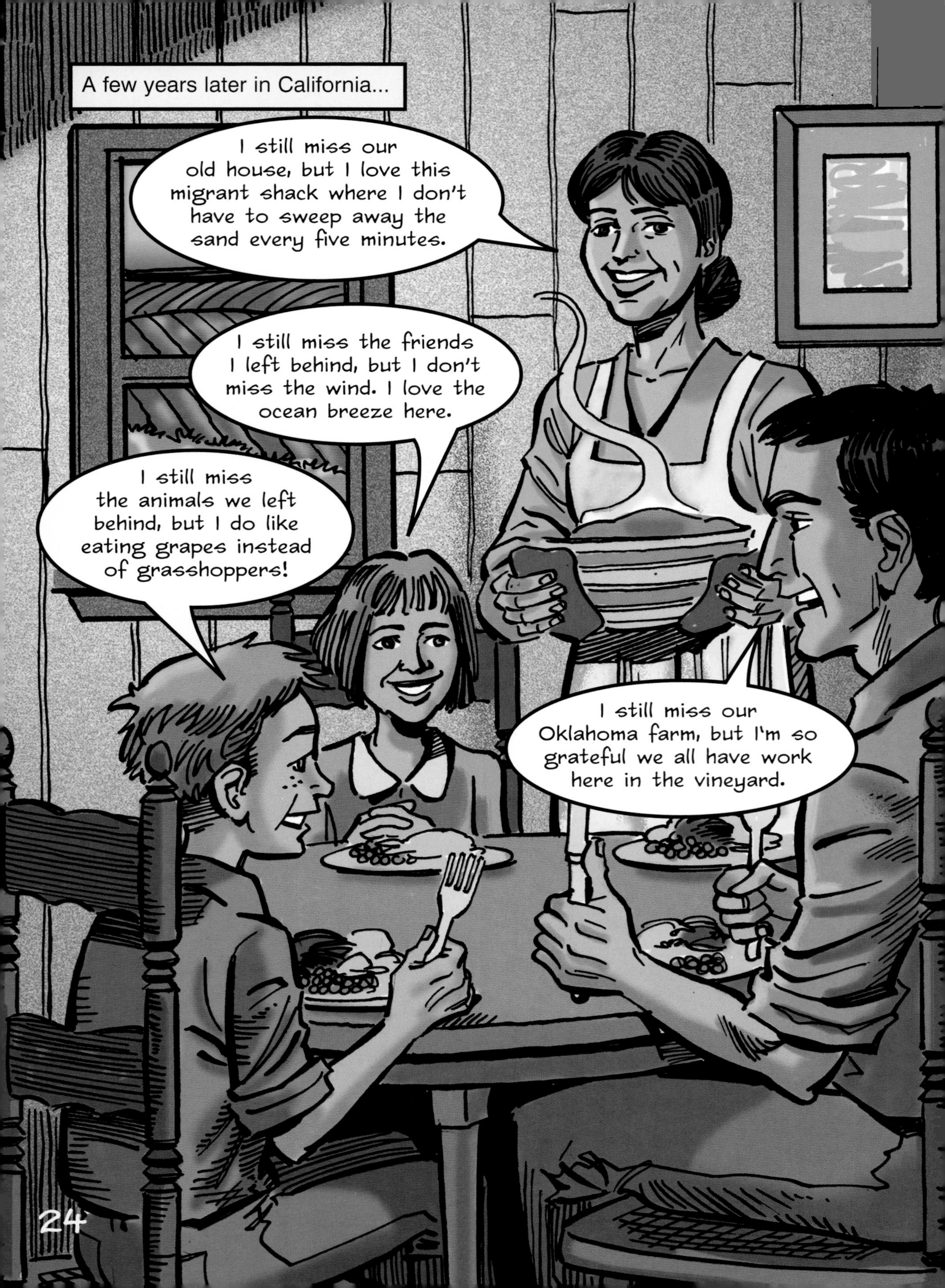
A few years later in California...
I still miss our old house, but I love this migrant shack where I don't have to sweep away the sand every five minutes.
I still miss the friends I left behind, but I don't miss the wind. I love the ocean breeze here.
I still miss the animals we left behind, but I do like eating grapes instead of grasshoppers!
I still miss our Oklahoma farm, but I'm so grateful we all have work here in the vineyard.

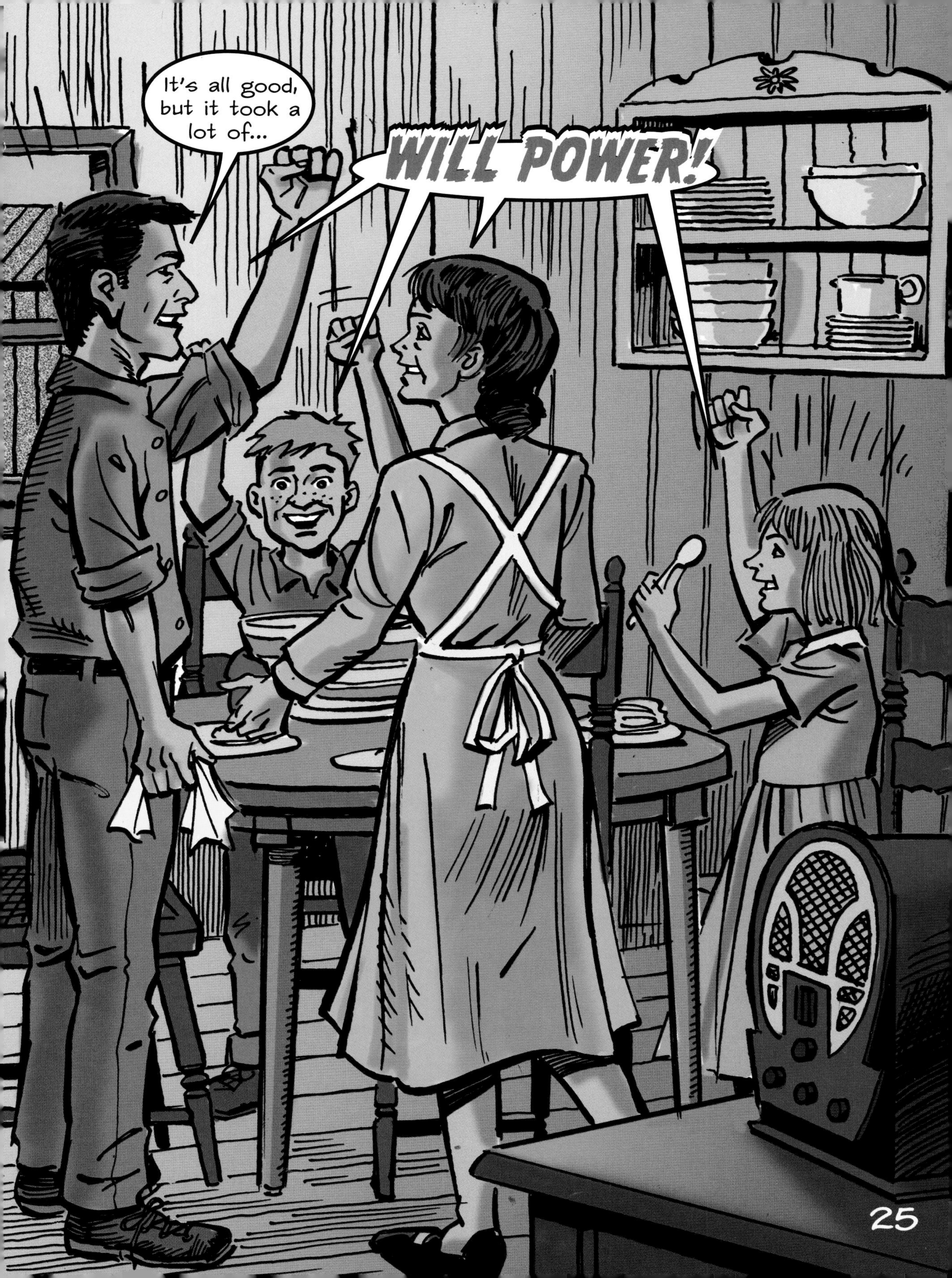
It's all good, but it took a lot of...
WILL POWER!

Q. **What caused the Dust Bowl?**

A. **Lack of knowledge about caring for the soil and a radical change in weather caused the Dust Bowl.**

Little food and lots of dust was hard on young children like this little boy who lived in Cimarron County, Oklahoma in 1936.

Explanation: In 1900, the Great Plains were lush with plants and grasses. During the Westward Movement, many families started farms on this rich soil. Rains brought abundant crops, and the farmers were delighted. But they did not know how to preserve the land, and erosion set in.

In 1930, the weather began to change. The rains stopped. The crops withered away. Heavy winds began to blow, lifting the dry soil in huge, gray clouds. There was no food for animals or people. There were no products to sell.

Q. What area was affected by the Dust Bowl?

A. People all through the Great Plains, from north to south, experienced this historic disaster.

Explanation: Although we think of Oklahoma and Texas as the Dust Bowl states, the drought was a much larger problem. It also extended to parts of New Mexico, Arkansas, Colorado, Kansas, Missouri, Wyoming, Nebraska, Iowa, South Dakota, North Dakota, Minnesota, Wisconsin, and Montana, as well as Manitoba and Saskatchewan, Canada.

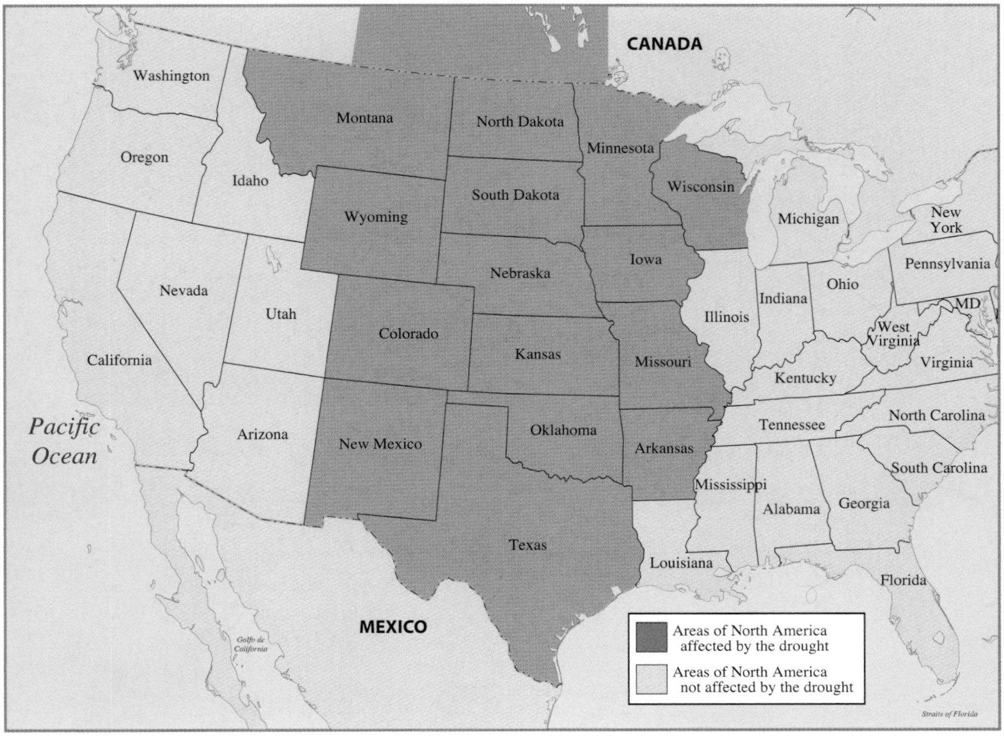
CANADA
Washington
Oregon
Idaho
Montana
North Dakota
Minnesota
Wisconsin
South Dakota
Wyoming
Michigan
New York
Pennsylvania
Nevada
Utah
Iowa
Nebraska
Ohio
Indiana
Illinois
MD
West Virginia
Virginia
California
Colorado
Kansas
Missouri
Kentucky
Tennessee
North Carolina
Pacific Ocean
Arizona
New Mexico
Oklahoma
Arkansas
South Carolina
Mississippi
Alabama
Georgia
Texas
Louisiana
Florida
MEXICO
Golfo de California
Areas of North America affected by the drought
Areas of North America not affected by the drought
Straits of Florida

Q. **How long did the Dust Bowl last?**

A. **The Dust Bowl lasted for nine years.**

Explanation: From 1930 to 1939, nearly a decade, thousands and thousands of people suffered the ravages of this natural and man-made catastrophe.

Some people called the 1930s, the Dirty Thirties. This farmer and his sons from Cimarron County, Oklahoma would probably agree with the nickname.

Q. How many people fled the Great Plains during the Dust Bowl?

A. Twenty-five percent of the population fled during the Dust Bowl.

Explanation: Although some traveled to California in hopes of a better life, 75 percent of the families stayed through these difficult times to keep their land and homes. They lost crops and animals, but they persevered until the skies opened in 1939, bringing rain and new life to the Great Plains once again.

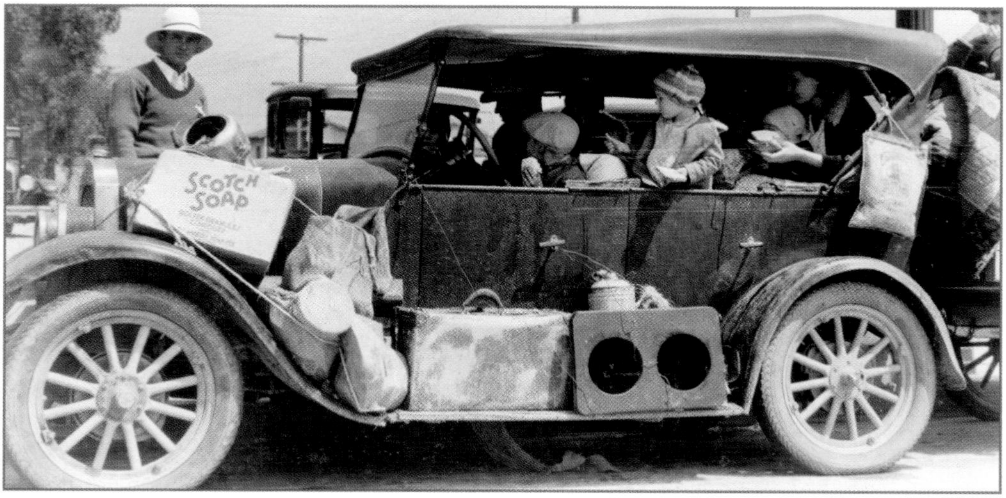
SCOTCH SOAP

Not all people who left the drought stricken areas of the country traveled by wagon. Some made the journey in cars. This family originally from Oklahoma, arrives in Bakersfield, California.

Glossary

caravan (ka-ruh-VAN): This is a group of wagons traveling together.

desperate (DESS-pur-it): When someone is in real trouble, they are desperate.

drought (DROUT): This means dryness or lack of rain.

meager (MEE-gur): This means small.

migrate (MYE-grate): To migrate is to relocate or to move away.

Panhandle of Oklahoma (PAN-han-duhl OHV OH-kluh-HOME-uh): This is a narrow strip of land in the northwest corner of Oklahoma.

preserve (pri-ZURV): This means to keep something in good condition.

relief (ri-LEEF): This is the easing of a problem.

Index

Websites

www.pbs.org/wgbh/amex/dustbowl

library.thinkquest.org/TQ0312210/Dustbowl.html

www.ccccok.org/museum/dustbowl.html

www.milforded.org/schools/foran/acesare/wq/index.html

About the Author

Jo Cleland is a survivor of the Dust Bowl. She was born in North Dakota in July 1936, when the thermometer read 121° F, the highest on record for the state. Today, Jo loves to write books, compose songs, and make games for kids.

About the Illustrator

Pete McDonnell is an illustrator who has worked worked in his field for twenty-four years. He has been creating comics, storyboards, and pop-art style illustration for clients such as Marvel Comics, the History Channel, Microsoft, Nestle, Sega, and many more. He lives in Sonoma County, California with his wife Shannon (also an illustrator) and son Jacob.